YOUR THUMPING HEART and BATTLING

blood system

FIND OUT HOW YOUR BODY WORKS!

Paul Mason

WAYLAND
www.waylandbooks.co.uk

CONTENTS

HUMAN BODY BASICS 3

YOUR THUMPING HEART 4

HEART PARTS 6

WHAT MAKES A HEART BEAT? 8

BLOOD (AND IRON) 10

WHAT COLOUR IS YOUR BLOOD? 12

TYPES OF BLOOD 14

BLOOD VESSELS 16

THE BODY'S DELIVERY SERVICE ... 18

THE BODY'S GARBAGE SERVICE 20

DEFENCE AGAINST MICROBE ATTACKS... 22

YOUR CIRCULATION – OUT OF THIS WORLD... 24

HELPING HEARTS 26

MAINTENANCE AND SERVICING 28

HEARTY WORDS! 30

HEARTY INFORMATION 31

INDEX 32

HUMAN BODY BASICS

What is an organism? Well, you are one, and so are gerbils, giraffes, porcupines and palm trees – living things are classed as organisms. To identify an organism you need to look out for seven 'life processes': breathing, eating, excreting, growing, moving, feeling and reproduction.

Cells

Each living organism is made of tiny building blocks called cells. There are more than 37 trillion cells in your body! Each cell is made to do a particular job, but they each have the same basic parts.

Tissue

Cells with the same function are joined together in a sheet called a tissue. Different tissues join together and form organs.

Organs and systems

Each organ in your body does a particular job, and each works together with other organs to create systems. Body systems take care of the life processes, such as breathing, digesting food and moving around.

Your heart is made of specialised cells called cardiac muscle cells.

Heart tissue is made of millions of cardiac muscle cells connected together.

Your heart is made of cardiac muscle tissue. It is the main organ in your circulatory system.

Your circulatory system runs through your whole body, delivering oxygen and nutrients, and taking away waste products.

3

YOUR THUMPING HEART

Press two fingertips onto your inner wrist, beneath your thumb. Feel that pulse? It's caused by your heartbeat. Every pulse equals one beat. And in your lifetime, your heart beats A LOT: almost 100,000 times a day, 35 million times a year, and 2.5 BILLION times in an entire life.

Pumping machine

Your heart's job is to pump blood around your body. The blood transports the oxygen and nutrients the body needs. The blood also carries away waste products. This is essential to keep you alive.

Luckily, your heart is REALLY good at pumping blood. An average adult's heart pumps over 7,500 litres of blood a day. It even generates its own electricity to keep itself going!

Boys v. girls

Boys' hearts are usually bigger than girls' by about 20% because their body size is generally bigger. Partly to make up for their smaller size, female hearts pump faster, at an average of roughly 78 beats per minute for adults, compared to an adult male's 70 beats. People who are especially fit have a slower heartbeat. Their hearts are stronger, so can pump more blood with each beat. Some athletes have a heartbeat as low as 30 beats per minute, or even fewer.

DID YOU KNOW?

Hearts work without their owners.

Human hearts have their own electrical system, so they can carry on beating even when separated from the body! They just need a blood supply, plus the right conditions to keep their cells alive.

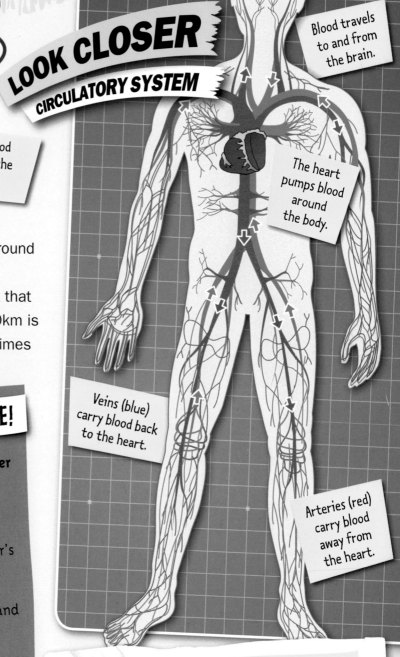

Blood travels to and from the brain.

The heart pumps blood around the body.

Veins (blue) carry blood back to the heart.

Arteries (red) carry blood away from the heart.

Laid end to end, your blood vessels would go around the world almost 2.5 times!

Blood and blood vessels

The blood pumped by the heart travels around the human body in a network of almost 100,000km of blood vessels. If you think that seems a long way, you're right – 100,000km is just a teeny bit less than two-and-a-half times around the world.

DON'T TRY THIS AT HOME!

In 1929, a German surgeon called Werner Forssmann decided to do an experiment.

Forssmann pushed a bendy tube into one of the veins in his own arm. After about 60cm of tube had gone in, the end had reached Werner's heart. He had invented a new way of giving patients drugs. Werner was later awarded the Nobel Prize for Medicine. He lived a long life and died at the age of 74 – of heart failure.

Werner Forssmann

See for yourself

In normal use a healthy heart NEVER gets tired – despite beating roughly once a second for every second of your life. Try squeezing a tennis ball once a second for a minute or two: you will start to see how amazing this is!

HEART PARTS

Stick a finger in each of your ears, so that you completely block out sound. You should still be able to hear something: ber-dum; ber-dum; ber-dum. It's your heart pumping blood around your body.

Pumping blood

Your heart is a great big ball of muscle. It pumps blood by contracting and relaxing in a complicated sequence. The noise you can hear is blood moving between different parts of the heart, as it works to circulate blood around your body.

DON'T TRY THIS AT HOME!

Before 1925, if you had a problem with the valve between the upper and lower chambers of your heart, you usually died.

In Britain, a Dr Souttar thought he could change this. He cut a hole in a patient's heart and stuck his finger inside to try and free up the valve. When Dr Souttar's bosses heard about the operation, they told him it was too dangerous and he mustn't do it again.

Four parts to each heart

Your heart has two sides, left and right. Each side is a separate pump. Each pump has two chambers, upper and lower, so the heart has four chambers in total. Strong valves separate the chambers; they open only to let blood flow from the upper chamber to the lower chamber.

Arteries and veins

Your heart is connected to the circulatory system by arteries and veins. Arteries take blood away from the heart. Veins bring it back. Arteries, veins and smaller blood vessels are organised into two networks. One carries blood to and from your lungs. The other carries blood to and from the rest of your body.

LOOK CLOSER
HEART PARTS

Heart parts are named 'left' or 'right' depending on whether they are on the left or right side of your body.

Hearts are not on the left.

Many people think your heart is only on the left side of your body. It's actually in the middle, but tilted slightly left. Because of this, your left lung has to be slightly smaller than your right lung.

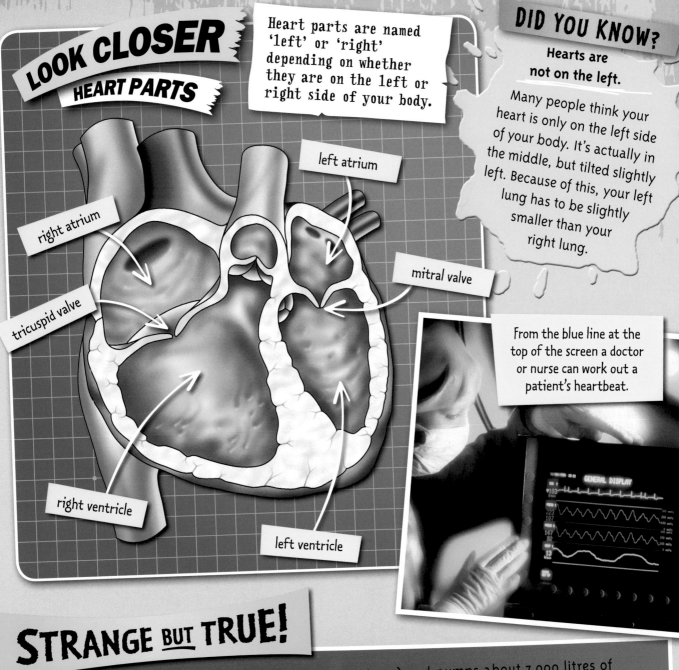

left atrium

right atrium

mitral valve

tricuspid valve

right ventricle

left ventricle

From the blue line at the top of the screen a doctor or nurse can work out a patient's heartbeat.

GENERAL DISPLAY

STRANGE BUT TRUE!

The blue whale has the largest heart of any animal. Each minute, it beats about five times (compared to an adult human's 70 times) and pumps about 7,000 litres of blood (compared to the human's 5.6 litres).

human to same scale

WHAT MAKES A HEART BEAT?

Have you heard the story of Frankenstein's monster – a creature stitched together from spare body parts, brought to life with a massive electric shock? It might surprise you to know that you have something in common with the monster. Without electricity, your heart (and therefore YOU) wouldn't be alive.

Shocking

Your heart is controlled by what is sometimes called 'nature's pacemaker'. Its proper name is the sinoatrial node – or SA node for short. The SA node is part of your heart's wall, and it sends an electric signal that triggers each heartbeat. The signal starts a complicated process of muscle contractions that control a one-way mechanism of valves opening and closing.

A one-way system

The valves between the upper and lower chambers of your heart work only one way. They open to allow blood to move down into the lower chambers, the ventricles. Then the valves close, making it impossible for blood to move back to where it came from.

As well as the valves within your heart, there are valves at the exits to the arteries that carry blood away. Together, these valves (and others like them in your blood vessels) make sure that your circulatory system is one-way only.

See for yourself

You can check how fast your heart is beating by taking your pulse. To do this, press your first and middle finger against the inside of your other wrist, at the base of your thumb. Count how many times you feel a throb in 20 seconds. Multiply this by 3 to get heartbeats per minute. This is your 'heart rate'.

LOOK CLOSER
HEARTBEATS

blood from body

blood from lungs

valves open

blood to body

blood to lungs

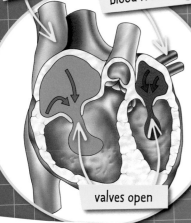

valves open

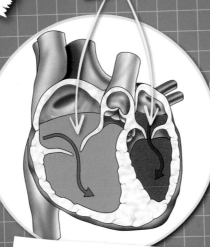

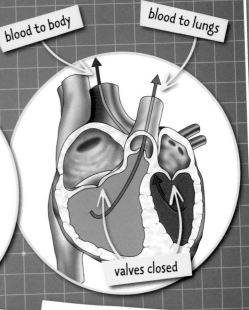

valves closed

1 When the heart is relaxed, blood enters the heart's upper chambers (atria) and lower chambers (ventricles).

2 The atria contract, forcing the remaining blood through the valves into the ventricles.

3 The ventricles contract, forcing blood into the circulatory system.

STRANGE BUT TRUE!

Your pulse rate gets slower as you grow up.

During childhood you grow quickly. Your heart beats fast, circulating nutrients and oxygen. Once you are fully grown, it beats more slowly.

Typical pulse rates

Newborn:	130
1 year:	120
6 years:	100
12 years:	85
Adult:	60-75

The human heart is covered in a layer of fat, which makes it look yellow. Underneath the fat, hearts are a clay colour.

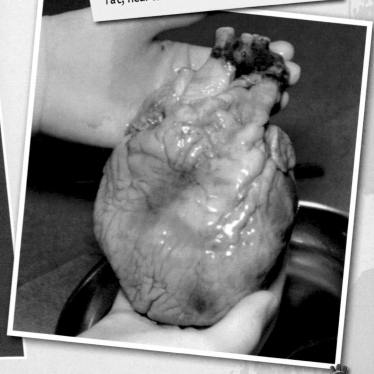

BLOOD (AND IRON)

Your blood is powerful stuff (despite being mostly water). For a start, it has a distinct smell. A great white shark can detect a few drops in the sea from up to 5km away. Up close, the smell of blood is strong enough for even humans to notice.

Red blood cells

The smell of blood is often described as metallic – which is no accident. The red cells in your blood are made mostly of a protein called haemoglobin, which contains iron. The iron helps your red blood cells transport oxygen around the body. This is an important job – without oxygen, your body quickly shuts down and dies.

You can guess how important red blood cells are by the number your body produces. Every day, an adult produces about 200 BILLION (to be more exact, 207,360,000,000) new red blood cells.

Other parts of your blood

Although it's red, your blood is not made only of red cells. It has three other important parts:

✳ **White cells** are your body's doctors. They fight infections, helping to keep your body safe from diseases and microscopic intruders. White cells are good, but they can be annoying – when you get a zit, it's because a bunch of white cells have got together to fight an infection in your skin.

STRANGE BUT TRUE!

Human blood is red because it contains iron. A horseshoe crab's blood contains copper instead — so horseshoe crabs have blue blood!

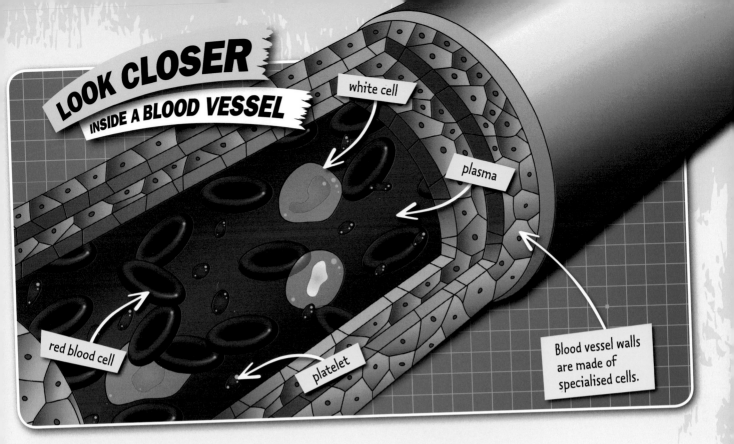

LOOK CLOSER
INSIDE A BLOOD VESSEL

white cell

plasma

red blood cell

platelet

Blood vessel walls are made of specialised cells.

* **Platelets** are tiny cell fragments that gather around a cut to form a clot and stop any bleeding.

* **Plasma** makes up 55% of blood and is mostly water. It carries the platelets, red cells and white cells (plus nutrients and other chemicals) around your body.

DON'T TRY THIS AT HOME!

In the 1660s, scientists experimented with taking the blood of one dog and putting it into another.

Few of the dogs survived. By 1818, Dr James Blundell had started performing blood transfusions on humans. Few of his patients survived.

It would be the 1900s before people worked out why this was happening — find out more on page 15.

See for yourself

YOU CAN MAKE A BLOOD-LIKE MIXTURE TO HAVE A LOOK AT ALL THE DIFFERENT PARTS.

* Take a small clear bowl and half fill it with a mixture of two-thirds syrup, one-third warm water and a couple of drops of red food colouring.

* Then add a handful of red Skittles, a single mint imperial, and a teaspoon of hundreds-and-thousands.

* Mix the mixture until it turns red!

The syrup mixture is the plasma, the Skittles are red blood cells, the mint is a white blood cell, and the hundreds-and-thousands are platelets!

(You can swap the sweets for any you find that are a similar colour and shape.)

WHAT COLOUR IS YOUR BLOOD?

Human blood is red, obviously! But whether your blood is bright red or dark red depends on where it is in your body, and what it's been doing.

Fetching and carrying

Blood gets its colour from a chemical reaction between the iron in your red blood cells and the oxygen they carry. Blood that is carrying more oxygen is brighter red. Blood that has got rid of most of its oxygen is a deep, dark red.

Where is blood brightest?

Your blood is brightest red when it has collected a fresh supply of oxygen from your lungs. It travels to the left side of the heart ready to be pumped to the rest of your body. The red blood cells deliver oxygen all over the body. The blood also collects and re-distributes nutrients from your digestive system, and other chemicals wherever they are needed.

LOOK CLOSER
BLOOD CELL COLOUR

A red blood cell carrying lots of oxygen.

A red blood cell with little oxygen and carrying waste products.

Where is blood darkest?

Blood is darkest on its journey from the right side of the heart to the lungs. This blood has got little oxygen and is loaded down with waste products, particularly carbon dioxide (CO_2) gas. These are released at the lungs, where the red blood cells collect more oxygen and return to the left side of the heart.

brain

Oxygenated blood is shown in red.

Deoxygenated blood is shown in blue.

Deoxygenated blood is pumped to the lungs where it collects oxygen.

Oxygenated blood is pumped to the arms, neck, head and brain.

lungs

heart

Deoxygenated blood is pumped back to the heart.

Oxygenated blood is pumped to the chest, lower body and legs

STRANGE BUT TRUE!

Bruises happen when your body gets a whack and tiny blood vessels are crushed. They start leaking blood, which is why a bruise starts off as a reddish-brown colour.

As the blood vessels repair, and the leaked blood is taken away, the bruise changes colour — first to purple, then green or yellow, and finally light yellow or brown.

Ouch! You can make out the damaged blood vessels.

TYPES OF BLOOD

Not all blood is the same. For a start, some people have a protein called Rh in their blood. Rh is short for 'rhesus'. The protein gets its name from being first discovered in rhesus monkeys.

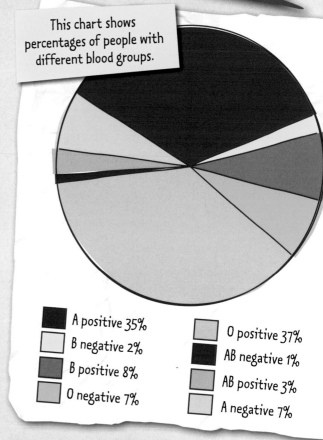

This chart shows percentages of people with different blood groups.

- A positive 35%
- B negative 2%
- B positive 8%
- O negative 7%
- O positive 37%
- AB negative 1%
- AB positive 3%
- A negative 7%

rhesus monkeys

Positive and negative

There's a good chance that the blood in your circulatory system has the Rh protein. Blood with the Rh protein is described as 'positive'. Roughly four in five people have positive blood. Blood without the Rh protein is called 'negative'.

Positive or negative is not the only difference between people's blood. Other proteins also decide whether your blood is in groups A, B, AB or O. In total there are eight different blood groups.

How much blood can a human lose?

Sometimes, an accident or illness causes people to lose blood. Most people could lose about 15% of their blood without any serious harm. Any more and the person would start to feel dizzy, cold, irritable, or all three.

Losing more than 30% of your blood makes it difficult for blood to get back to your heart, which can be fatal. Losing 50% or more will almost certainly cause death.

Matching blood types

For anyone who loses a lot of blood, today it is possible to transfer blood safely from one person to another. This is called a transfusion. The blood comes from volunteers, who have donated their blood so that it can be stored until it is needed. They are called blood donors.

Not everyone's blood suits everyone else. O-negative blood can be given to anyone, so people with this blood type are often called universal donors. But people from some blood groups need blood from exactly the same group.

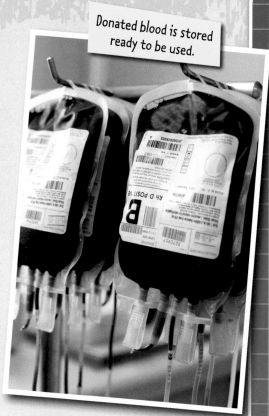

Donated blood is stored ready to be used.

STRANGE BUT TRUE!

Humans have four basic blood types (A, B, AB, O), and so do dogs. Cats have 11 different blood types, which seems plenty — until you realise that cows have EIGHT HUNDRED.

DID YOU KNOW?

Your blood group DOESN'T determine your personality.

In Japan, many people think your blood type determines your personality. They ask 'What's your blood type?' the same way other people ask, 'What's your star sign?' There is no evidence that your blood group DOES actually influence your personality.

An average adult has around 5 litres of blood in their body. When you donate blood, your body makes more.

1 LITRE

1 LITRE

1 LITRE

1 LITRE

1 LITRE

BLOOD VESSELS

Look at a nearby adult. Inside that adult are a lot of blood vessels, carrying blood around their body. In fact, if you laid the blood vessels in a line, they would stretch a quarter of the distance to the Moon.

Blood vessels

Every time your heart beats, it pumps blood around this huge network of blood vessels. There are three basic types of blood vessel: arteries, veins and capillaries.

✳ Arteries These take blood away from the heart. The blood inside an artery is under high pressure – so high, in fact, that if a tiny hole is made in an artery, the blood is said to squirt out up to 9m with every heartbeat.

✳ Veins These bring blood back to the heart. The blood that is a long way from the heart is under less pressure.

So veins often contain valves (like the ones in the heart, see page 8) to make sure the blood does not go backwards.

✳ Capillaries These tiny blood vessels connect the bigger blood vessels to the rest of the body. Their walls allow gas, liquid and chemicals to pass through them, and into other parts of your body. As blood passes through the capillaries it delivers oxygen and collects waste.

Blood leaves the heart in arteries. These divide into a network of tiny capillaries. These then link together to form veins, which carry deoxygenated blood back to the heart and lungs.

LOOK CLOSER
BLOOD VESSELS

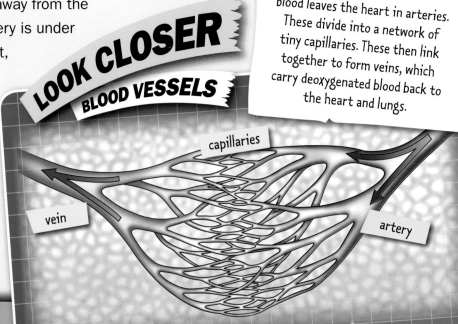

capillaries

vein

artery

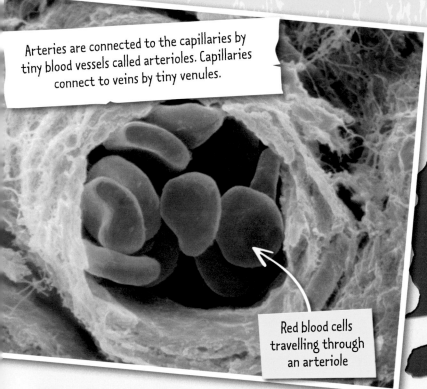

Arteries are connected to the capillaries by tiny blood vessels called arterioles. Capillaries connect to veins by tiny venules.

Red blood cells travelling through an arteriole

DID YOU KNOW?

Your cornea has no blood vessels.

The cornea is a clear layer at the very front of your eye. Even tiny blood vessels inside it would get in the way of your vision, so the cornea has no blood supply of its own. Instead it gets oxygen directly from the air, and nutrients from tears and clear fluid.

Blood pressure

When people on medical dramas shout out phrases like '140 over 90', they are talking about the patient's blood pressure – how strongly their blood is passing through the circulatory system. If the blood is not circulating strongly enough, the body will slowly be starved of oxygen and nutrients, and overloaded with carbon dioxide.

The first number is maximum blood pressure, which is recorded when blood is pumped out of the heart. The second number is the patient's minimum blood pressure, recorded when the heart relaxes and fills with with blood.

DON'T TRY THIS AT HOME!

William Harvey (1578–1657) was the first scientist to understand the circulation of blood in our bodies.

Harvey was a great scientist – but if you were an animal, it was probably best to steer clear of his workroom. He would experiment on just about anything: eels, fish, chicks, pigeons and even shrimps were among the surprising creatures Harvey sliced up to see how they worked.

STRANGE BUT TRUE!

Drinking coffee or energy drinks containing caffeine raises your blood pressure. But, having a pet dog or cat has been shown to lower people's blood pressure!

THE BODY'S DELIVERY SERVICE

Your blood system is a bit like a non-stop delivery service for your body. Every second you're alive, your circulatory system collects and delivers food, oxygen and other important items, such as hormones, wherever they are needed.

Crucial capillaries

Collection and delivery is done by your capillaries. These tiny blood vessels have small openings in their walls, which allow chemicals to pass to and from the blood.

In the lungs, for example, capillaries wrap themselves around tiny air sacs called alveoli. As the blood flows past, oxygen passes from the alveoli into the capillaries through the vessel wall. It then flows into larger blood vessels for transport around the body. When this blood reaches a muscle or another body part in need of oxygen, the oxygen is released and passes into the body cells.

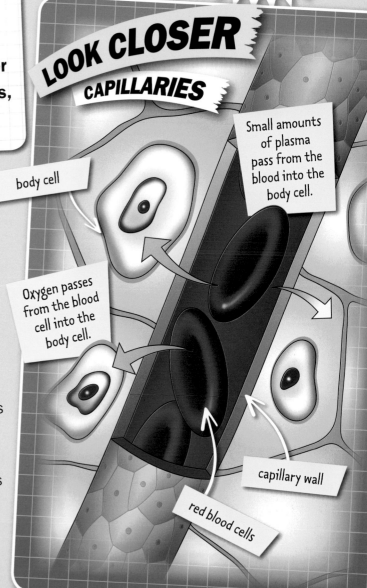

LOOK CLOSER

CAPILLARIES

body cell

Small amounts of plasma pass from the blood into the body cell.

Oxygen passes from the blood cell into the body cell.

capillary wall

red blood cells

More energy needed

As well as oxygen, blood delivers nutrients around the body. If you go running, for example, your muscles use up their stored energy. They signal to your brain that more is needed. Your brain tells your lungs to breathe harder, and your heart to beat faster. Your blood picks up more nutrients from your digestive system and transports them to the muscles.

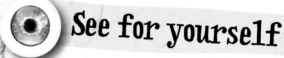
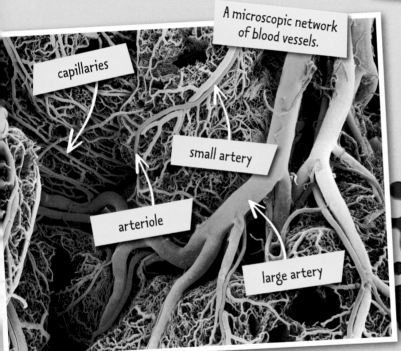

A microscopic network of blood vessels.

capillaries

small artery

arteriole

large artery

A side order of hormones

As well as oxygen and nutrients, your circulatory system delivers hormones. These are chemical messengers that tell different parts of your body how to behave. For example, hormones control when you go to sleep, grow, feel hungry – and even how fast your heart beats.

Hormones can affect your mood – making you happy, sad, angry or annoyed.

THE BODY'S GARBAGE SERVICE

As well as being a delivery service, your circulatory system also does non-stop rubbish collection. It takes away waste and by-products that the body no longer needs. Getting rid of these requires help from the lungs and two crucial little organs: the kidneys.

Expelling poison gas

When your muscles burn energy, one of the by-products is a gas called carbon dioxide, or CO_2. Large amounts of this gas can be poisonous to humans so your body needs to get rid of it quickly! Fortunately, blood that has delivered its oxygen to the muscles has space to take on waste products. The CO_2 is transported to the lungs for us to breathe out.

Two million tiny blood filters

At any one moment, almost 25% of the blood leaving your heart is heading for your kidneys to be cleaned. When the blood arrives, it is fed into the renal pyramids. These are full of tiny, looping tubes called nephrons. Each nephron is a separate blood filter, and you have about one million nephrons per kidney.

All those nephrons are constantly cleaning your blood, putting the waste into urine. The urine moves down a tube called the ureter, from the kidney to your bladder. This is a sac with muscular walls, where the urine is stored. Once the bladder is full, your brain sends a warning that it's time to pass urine.

An underwater swimmer blows out CO_2.

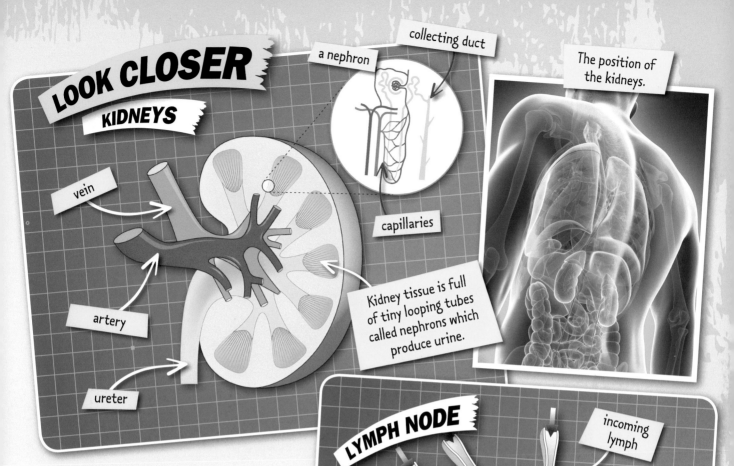

a nephron

collecting duct

capillaries

The position of the kidneys.

vein

artery

ureter

Kidney tissue is full of tiny looping tubes called nephrons which produce urine.

LYMPH NODE

incoming lymph

outgoing lymph

Inside the lymph node, lymph is filtered and white blood cells fight any germs that might make you unwell.

vein

artery

The lymph system

The kidneys aren't your only clean-up crew. Your body also comes equipped with a drainage network called the lymph system. This collects fluid, known as lymph, from all around the body. The fluid is forced through tiny structures called lymph nodes, which filter out impurities.

The lymph system also helps your body fight disease. The lymph nodes add disease-fighting white blood cells to the blood. They also contain macrophages – specialised blood cells that can destroy unwanted particles, such as germs.

STRANGE BUT TRUE!

When empty, an adult's bladder is about the size and shape of a pear. When full, it can hold around 500ml – that's about the same volume as a small water bottle.

DEFENCE AGAINST MICROBE ATTACKS

Your body is constantly under attack! Tiny organisms called microbes are always trying to get inside. There are A LOT of them, too – you probably have more microbes just on your hand than there are people on Earth.

Many microbes

Not all microbes are harmful. Microbes in your intestine provide you with healthy vitamins, for example. But some microbes are dangerous. If they manage to get inside you, they can cause sickness. One example is a type of microbe called a virus. Viruses cause diseases ranging from ordinary colds or warts, to measles and chicken pox.

Fortunately, your body has a good defence system against microbes – and your blood plays an important part.

Cuts and scabs

Your biggest defence against microbes is your skin, a barrier they cannot get through. Sometimes, though, your skin gets cut or grazed. Blood rushes to the spot. Platelets in the blood stick together like glue, forming a barrier. The barrier also contains other blood cells and thread-like material called fibrin. The fibrin helps to hold the barrier together as it forms into a scab. The scab forms a barrier while your skin and the tissue underneath heal.

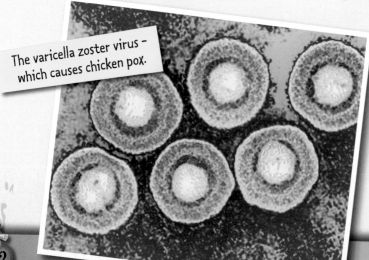

The varicella zoster virus – which causes chicken pox.

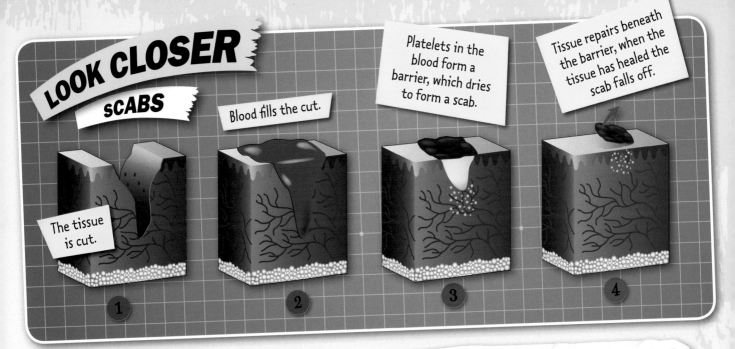

LOOK CLOSER

SCABS

The tissue is cut.

Blood fills the cut.

Platelets in the blood form a barrier, which dries to form a scab.

Tissue repairs beneath the barrier, when the tissue has healed the scab falls off.

1

2

3

4

White blood cells

If any microbes DO get into your body, white blood cells will attack them. They do this in two different ways:

✳ Some white cells surround and destroy things that shouldn't be in your body.

✳ Other white cells produce chemicals called antibodies, which fight microbe invaders – including viruses. Some are even able to remember particular types of virus. This helps them destroy the virus even more quickly next time it appears.

White blood cells are larger than red ones.

See for yourself

Just how small are viruses? Really VERY small.

To get an idea of how tiny viruses are compared to your body's normal cells, imagine that a virus is the size of a baseball. In comparison, your body's normal cells would each be the same size as the whole baseball field!

DON'T TRY THIS AT HOME!

The existence of viruses was first proved in 1901, by a US Army team working in Cuba.

The theory was that yellow fever might be spread by something carried by mosquitoes. To establish whether this was true, volunteers allowed themselves to be bitten by mosquitoes. Many of the volunteers DID develop yellow fever. Some members of the research team even died of the disease.

YOUR CIRCULATION

-OUT OF THIS WORLD

You might think that your circulatory system works pretty much the same way, wherever you are. You'd be wrong though – and to prove it, all you need to do is visit outer space. Just a few weeks aboard the International Space Station (ISS) should do it!

Designed for Earth

Your body is brilliantly designed for life on planet Earth. Leaving Earth has strange effects on the human body. One of the most important is that our bodies are fooled into producing less blood.

On Earth, gravity means that blood normally collects in your legs. This blood then has to fight gravity to get back up to your heart. In fact, it would have a hard time doing this without the valves in your leg veins, which are like a ladder for the blood moving up your legs.

An astronaut aboard the International Space Station.

1 On Earth, gravity pulls blood down into the legs.

2 In the low gravity of space, blood from the legs rises.

3 The body is fooled into thinking it suddenly contains more blood. It slowly adapts to the new conditions.

4 Returning to Earth, the body has to adapt to the effects of gravity.

Zero gravity

In space there's no gravity, so blood does not collect in your legs – it builds up in your chest and head instead. Your brain thinks your body contains too much blood overall. First, you get headaches and a puffy face. Then your heart gets bigger, to handle the extra blood flow it's expecting. At the same time, your heart becomes weaker because it does not have to fight gravity to pump blood up your body. In the end, your body starts to produce less blood.

YOU CAN'T TRY THIS AT HOME!

Astronauts sometimes faint, or experience 'grey-out' during takeoff.

This happens because gravity has trapped too much blood in their legs, so not enough reaches their brain. Astronauts may also faint when they return to Earth. After a long space visit, their heart isn't used to fighting gravity and struggles to get enough blood to their brain.

STRANGE BUT TRUE!

During a long stay in space, astronauts can lose up to a litre of fluid from EACH LEG. Without this fluid, your legs start to look thin and loose-skinned. This is sometimes called 'chicken legs'.

HELPING HEARTS

An adult's heart can beat almost 200 times a minute, for example during hard exercise. Normally it only needs to beat about 70 times. So, even someone whose heart is not working properly can do simple tasks quite easily. However, sometimes people develop heart problems that need treatment.

Heart problems among children

Roughly 1 in 100 babies are born with some kind of heart problem. Signs of a heart problem include finding it hard to get enough breath, chest pains, and an irregular heartbeat. Drugs, surgery or other medical treatment can often provide a cure. Most children with heart problems grow up to be healthy adults.

Improvements in treatment

Every year, new and better treatments are being developed for those with heart problems. For instance, someone with an irregular heartbeat might need a pacemaker – an electrical device that tells the heart when to beat. The first heart pacemakers were complicated devices that were painful for patients. Today, they are tiny battery-powered boxes that a surgeon places inside the chest and wires up to the heart.

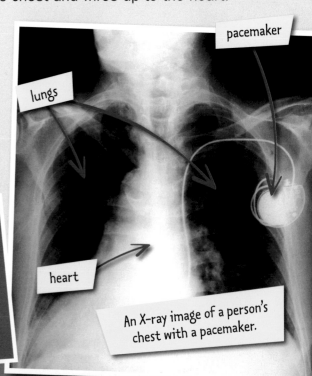

pacemaker

lungs

heart

An X-ray image of a person's chest with a pacemaker.

STRANGE BUT TRUE!

When heart pacemakers were first developed, today's tiny batteries were not available. The earliest pacemakers got their electricity from light fittings, wall sockets — and even a wind-up generator!

Heart surgery

If someone's heart is damaged or malformed in some way, it can often be fixed with an operation. This no longer involves the doctor cutting a hole and sticking his finger into the patient's heart (see page 6)! In fact, the latest heart operations are done using robots controlled by the surgeon. The robot can fit into smaller spaces and causes less damage to the surrounding tissue.

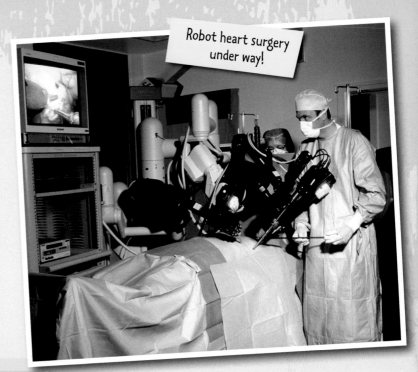

Robot heart surgery under way!

DON'T TRY THIS AT HOME!

The first-ever heart transplant happened in 1967. Louis Washkansky was given the heart of a young woman who had died in a car accident.

Despite the fact that Washkansky died 18 days later, surgeons considered the operation a success. Today, heart transplants are common. In the future, though, doctors may be able to fit people with mechanical hearts, which scientists have been developing since the 1950s.

Like all muscles, the heart needs a blood supply. If the coronary arteries around the heart become damaged or blocked then it will be harder for blood to reach the muscle tissue. If too little blood reaches the heart, the heartbeat may stutter or stop.

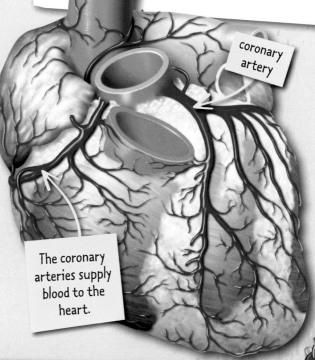

coronary artery

The coronary arteries supply blood to the heart.

DID YOU KNOW?

How much energy does it take to run a heart?

On average, your heart is estimated to use a minimum of 2.5 gigajoules of energy in your lifetime. That's enough to dry 232 loads of laundry in a clothes dryer!

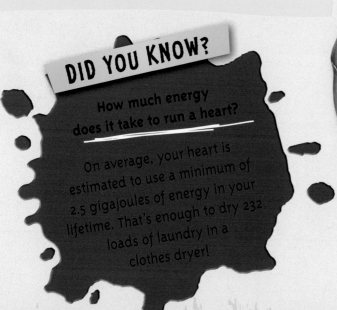

MAINTENANCE AND SERVICING

Your heart does a lot of good work for you. It delivers oxygen and other supplies; takes away your body's waste products; fights off infections and illnesses; and serves as a messaging service for different parts of your body to keep in touch. It stands to reason you want to look after it – but how?

Exercise is good for your heart.

① Run a little, every day

Actually, you don't have to run – just get active. Your heart is a muscle, and like any other muscle you can train it to be fitter by making it work harder. Aim to do 30 minutes of exercise five days a week – you need to be working hard enough to make you sweat.

② Don't start smoking

Smoking is really bad for your heart and circulation. It damages the lining of your arteries, causing them to narrow. The gases in tobacco smoke take up room in the blood leaving less space for oxygen. Tobacco smoke also contains drugs that affect your heart rate, making your heart work harder than normal.

③ Watch your weight

Being overweight places a strain on your heart. Being heavy is like carrying around a loaded backpack all the time. Your heart has to work harder to circulate blood to your lungs and muscles.

④ **Eat right**

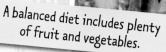

A balanced diet includes plenty of fruit and vegetables.

Avoid eating lots of fat: deep-fried chips (in fact, anything deep-fried); butter, cheese and cream; and sweet things such as biscuits, cakes and chocolate. Make sure you eat plenty of fruit and vegetables, and oily fish such as tuna, mackerel or sardines.

⑤ **Avoid extra salt**

Eating salt makes it harder for your kidneys to remove excess water from your blood. Instead, the water builds up – which puts a strain on your heart and blood vessels.

Oily fish such as mackerel contain a kind of good fat called omega-3. Experts think omega-3 may improve the health of your heart.

⑥ **Stressed? Walk or talk**

Stress – feeling worried – is often associated with heart problems. If you feel worried about something, go for a walk outside to relax. If that doesn't work, talk to someone about what's worrying you.

See for yourself

Lots of people like to listen to music while exercising. Exercise increases your heart rate - but can music do the same thing? Try this experiment to find out:

Listen to something slow and soppy for one minute. Take your pulse (see page 8 for how to do this).

Now listen to an upbeat party tune for one minute; take your pulse again.

Now compare results.

Was there a difference?

Talking with friends can help reduce worries.

HEARTY WORDS!

aorta artery that takes oxygenated blood from the heart to the rest of the body

blood pressure the physical force that pushes blood against the wall of a blood vessel

blood vessels tubes inside the body through which blood flows

cell the smallest building-block that a living thing can be made of, usually only visible under a powerful microscope

circulate move around in a constant loop

circulatory system a network of blood vessels that makes it possible for blood to flow around the body from the heart

coronary relating to the heart

fatal deadly

gravity the force of attraction between objects. Larger objects have greater gravity, so the Earth pulls objects towards itself more strongly than, for example, a tennis ball does.

heart contraction tightening or shortening of heart muscle to pump blood through the circulatory system

heart disease weakness in the blood vessels that supply the heart itself with blood

heart transplant operation in which a living person is given a new heart, donated by someone who has recently died

lymph nodes swellings that are part of the lymphatic system, here lymph fluid is filtered and white blood cells are formed to destroy harmful microbes

microbe a tiny organism made of just a single cell

nutrient food product that living things can use to survive, grow or repair themselves

obese overweight by an amount that is likely to affect health

oxygenated with oxygen added

pacemaker artificial device that tells the heart how often to beat

pulse single heartbeat, or the speed at which someone's heart is beating. A pulse of 63 means your heart is beating 63 times per minute.

receptor part of a cell within the human body that responds to a particular chemical signal

renal relating to the kidneys

transfusion transfer of blood into someone's body

valve in the heart or circulatory system, a valve is a one-way trapdoor that allows blood to pass before closing

vein blood vessel that brings blood to the heart

HEARTY INFORMATION

Are you hungry for extra information about your heart?
Here are some good places to find out more:

BOOKS TO READ

Truth or Busted: *The Fact or Fiction Behind Human Bodies,* Paul Mason, Wayland 2014

Infographic Top Ten: *Record-Breaking Humans,* Jon Richards and Ed Simkins, Wayland 2014

MindWebs: *Human Body,* Anna Claybourne, Wayland 2014

WEBSITES

http://kidshealth.org/kid/htbw/heart.html

This website is a really good place to find out all sorts of information about the human body. It has an excellent section on the heart.

http://www.childrensuniversity.manchester. ac.uk/interactives/science/exercise/heart/

The Children's University of Manchester, UK, has all sorts of information for kids, presented in the form of labelled illustrations. It includes some easily understood information about the heart and circulatory system, focusing on the benefits of exercise.

PLACES TO VISIT

In London, the **Science Museum** has regular exhibitions and displays explaining how the body works. The museum is at:

Exhibition Road
South Kensington
London SW7 2DD

The Science Museum also has a really good website:

www.sciencemuseum.org.uk/whoami/findoutmore/yourbrain.aspx

The **Natural History Museum** has an amazing 'Human Biology Gallery' where you can find out all about the blood and the jobs it does inside the human body. The museum is at:

The Natural History Museum
Cromwell Road
London
SW7 5BD

The museum also has a good website:

http://www.nhm.ac.uk/visit-us/galleries/blue-zone/human-biology/

INDEX

alveoli 18
animals 3, 7, 10, 11, 14, 15, 17
antibodies 23
aorta 16, 30
arteries 5, 6, 8, 16, 17, 19, 21, 26, 27, 28
arterioles 17, 19
athletes 4
atria 7, 9

bladder 20, 21
blood cells 10, 11, 12, 13, 17, 21, 22, 23
blood loss 14–15
blood pressure 17, 30
blood transfusions 11, 15, 30
blood types 14–15
blood vessels 5, 6, 8, 11, 13, 16–17, 18, 19, 29, 30
brain 5, 13, 19, 25
bruises 13

capillaries 16, 17, 18, 19, 21
carbon dioxide 13, 17, 20
cardiac muscle 3, 8
circulatory system 3, 5, 6, 8, 9, 14, 17, 18–19, 20–21, 24–25, 28, 30
clotting 11
cornea 17
cuts 11, 22

diet 26, 29
disease 10, 21, 23, 28

exercise 28, 29

fainting 25
Forssmann, Werner 5

gravity 24, 25, 30

haemoglobin 10, 13
Harvey, William 17
heart
  cells 3, 4
  chambers 6, 8, 9
  colour 9
  electrical system 4, 8
  failure 5
  size 4, 6, 7
  surgery 5, 6, 26, 27
  transplants 27, 30
heartbeat 4, 7, 8, 16, 19, 26, 27
hormones 19

infection 10, 28
iron 10, 12

kidneys 20–21, 25, 29

life processes 3
lungs 6, 7, 9, 12, 13, 16, 18, 19, 20, 28
lymph system 21

microbes 22–23, 30
muscles 18, 19, 20, 28

nutrients 3, 4, 9, 11, 12, 17, 19, 30

oxygen 3, 4, 9, 10, 12, 13, 16, 17, 18, 19, 20, 28

pacemakers 26, 30
plaque 26
plasma 11
platelets 11, 22
pulse 4, 8, 9, 29, 30

Rh protein 14

SA node 8
skin 23
space 24–25

valves 6, 7, 8, 9, 16, 24, 30
veins 5, 6, 16, 17, 21, 24
ventricles 7, 8, 9
venules 11
viruses 22, 23

waste products 3, 4, 12, 13, 16, 28

WAYLAND

First published in 2015 by Wayland

Copyright © Wayland 2015

Wayland
338 Euston Road
London NW1 3BH

Wayland Australia
Level 17/207
Kent Street
Sydney, NSW 2000

All rights reserved.

Editor: Annabel Stones
Designer: Rocket Design (East Anglia) Ltd
Consultant: John Clancy, Former Senior Lecturer in Applied Human Physiology
Proofreader: Susie Brooks

ISBN 978 0 7502 92405
Library eBook ISBN 978 0 7502 92412
Dewey categorisation: 612.1-dc23

Printed in China

10 9 8 7 6 5 4 3 2 1

Wayland, part of Hachette Children's Group and published by Hodder and Stoughton Limited
www.hachette.co.uk

Artwork: Ian Thompson: p7 tl, p16 b, p18; Ian Thompson/Stefan Chabluk: p5 tr, p9 t, p11 t; Stefan Chabluk: p12 bl, p13 l, p21 tl, p21 cr, p23 t, p25 t.

Picture acknowledgements: Getty: p5 bl Keystone/Stringer; NASA: p24; Science Photo Library: p7 cr JESSE, p9 br KLAUS GULDBRANDSEN, p17 tl ROFESSORS P.M. MOTTA & S. CORRER, p19 l SUSUMU NISHINAGA, p22 bl Cavallini James/BSIP, p27 t PASCAL GOETGHELUCK, p27 b ASKLEPIOS MEDICAL ATLAS; Shutterstock: Cover all, p3 t, p3 ct, p3 cb, p3 b, p4 tr, p5 tl, p5 br, p7 b whale, p7 b man, p8 bl, p10 tl, p10 br, p13 tr, p13 br, p14 tl, p15 tr, p15 r panel, p15 bl, p17 cr, p17 b eel, p17 b fish, p17 b pigeon, p19 r, p20, p21 tr, p21 b, p23 br, p23 bl, p25 br, p26, p28 cl, p28 cr, p28 br, p29 tr, p29 cr, p29 cl, p29 bl. Graphic elements from Shutterstock.

The website addresses (URLs) included in this book were valid at the time of going to press. However, it is possible that contents or addresses may have changed since the publication of this book. No responsibility for any such changes can be accepted by either the author or the Publisher.

YOUR BRILLIANT BODY

Marvel at the wonders of the human body with this fact-packed series.

978 0 7502 9388 4

978 0 7502 9246 7

978 0 7502 9240 5

978 0 7502 9237 5

978 0 7502 9249 8

978 0 7502 9243 6

Find out more about the human body with other Wayland titles:

978 0 7502 7868 3

978 0 7502 8158 4

978 0 7502 8241 3

978 0 7502 8280 2